Table of contents

<u>Getting more efficient on the inside</u>
<u>A final word</u>

Introduction

My first ebook on window-cleaning is "How to start your own window cleaning business...with an asset you already possess." It is called "How do I climb the ladder?" and it explains how ladders are used in cleaning windows from second stories on tall buildings.

It is still a chapter that I am proud of. It offers excellent advice about how to safely use ladders. To make ladders safer and more user-friendly, it lists some attachments that can be used in conjunction with them. The article describes a modern ladder that converts from an A-frame ladder to an extension ladder.

It is, however, the most outdated, outmoded and possibly misleading chapter in the entire book. What if a window washer doesn't have to use a ladder? Imagine if they could do without a ladder. They can use a water-fed pole to do this, not just for buildings with 2 stories, but also for buildings up to 4 stories tall. Window cleaners can eliminate ladders for many jobs. In some cases, they can even get rid of cherry pickers or scissor lifts.

I was so excited to finally use water-fed poles. Why did ladders take me so long to learn? Why did I spend so long doing things the hard-way?

Even as a window cleaner, I was familiar with water-fed poles. But I didn't bother to look into them.

It is difficult to clean windows. I was shocked to discover that you could clean second-story windows by simply standing on the ground with a water-fed pole. External windows often need to be cleaned with a sharp knife. Then I thought, how can one clean a second-story window that is stained with water using a brush?

It? It seemed absurd to me.

When I was giving a quote, the blurb I used included the following statement: "For high windows, I endeavor to use a ladder, instead of relying on a pole so that I can get up close to them." This meant that I didn't rush or do things half-heartedly. Water-fed poles, to me, were basic tools meant for home handymen who wanted to try their hand at cleaning windows that they couldn't reach. I did not know there were water-fed poles that could be used for professional or industrial purposes. They were not available at the cleaning supply shop I frequented. Now I know water-fed poles can be used to clean windows.

Why did I change my mind? Another window cleaner is responsible for my mind-shifting. Saleem Khan is the name of this man and he is also the one to whom this book was dedicated. He was a friend of mine and I often referred him to work. He was telling me about his experience with a water-fed pole and extolling the benefits of not having to use a ladder. He insisted that the pole was effective at cleaning windows, despite my doubts.

Although I needed more proof, I was open to the idea. Saleem offered to help me with a job, use his pole and give me the chance to test it. I was stunned. It was amazing how fast the windows were cleaned. It was also amazing how well it cleaned windows up to 2nd floor. The rest is history. We made arrangements for Saleem, who helped me buy my own unit.

This book is about the lessons I've learned from this history. It is not a long story. Although I have only used a water-fed pole for a short time, I have learned a lot.

Chapter 1 –The conventional method

I have written an ebook about window cleaning, as I already mentioned. I described only one method of cleaning windows in my book, and I called it "the basic method." This chapter will discuss the same method. It will be contrasted with the water-fed pole method in this book.

You will probably be a window washer and know a lot about it. Even if you're not a window washer, it is worth learning about it. Even though you may end up using a waterfed pole to clean external windows, it will not work on internal ones. To clean internal windows, you will need to use the traditional method. You may also need to apply it to external windows if your water-fed pole is damaged or malfunctions.

Below are the steps of the traditional method as illustrated in my ebook.

<u>STEP 1: Scrub the window</u>

First, fill your bucket with detergent and water. Next, place the strip washer in the bucket. Once the strip washer is wet, you can use it to clean the window. It doesn't have to be pressed very hard against your window, especially if the scraper will be used next. The window's cleanliness will determine how hard you press the strip washer. You can also adjust the pressure according to how easy certain marks are removed.

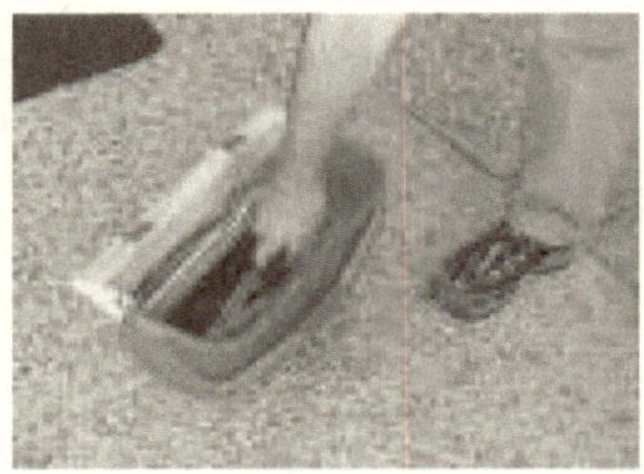

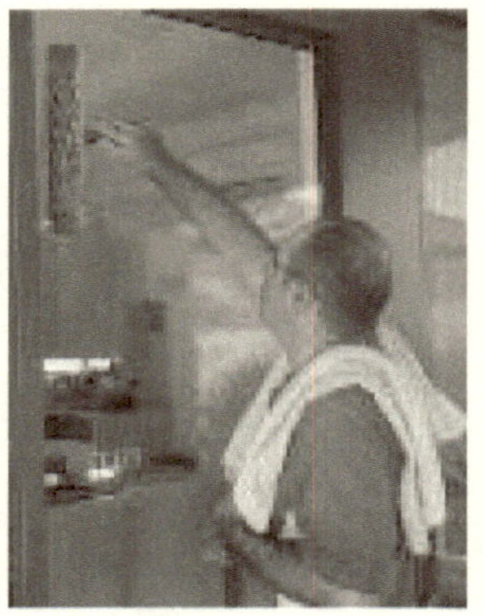

<u>STEP 2 – Scrape the window</u>

    The next step is to use the scraper. Scrape the window with a series of straight horizontal or vertical strokes. Make sure you use a new sharp blade. A good rule to follow is new house = new blade. Only scrape a window that is wet.

STEP 4 – Dry 2 edges: top and side

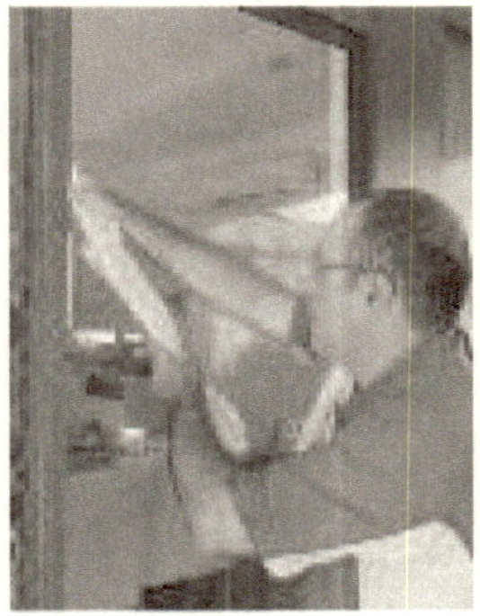

Dry 2 edges of the window. It is best to dry the top edge and one of the side edges. You will be starting your squeegee strokes from these dry edges, to minimise and chance of leaving water streaks behind your squeegee.

Your squeegee must be dry. Use a rag to dry the squeegee. One I
have around my waist is specifically for drying the squeegee.
The squeegee can be used horizontally or vertically to run across the
glass. You should start in the corner where both edges have been
dried with your towel. This is how I am running the squeegee
vertically along the window. Dry your squeegee once more after the
first stroke. A second stroke is usually required, as it is here. You
should choose a squeegee that is as efficient as possible when you're

working on a window. You are unlikely to find a squeegee that is exactly the same height as the window. It is unlikely that one of your squeegees will be exactly the same height or width as the window. This depends on whether the squeegee will be used horizontally or vertically. You can use two strokes to get the job done. The second stroke will only take about half the time and the squeegee can still cover the same area. You'll see that I used a smaller squeegee to make my second stroke. This was so that the majority of the squeegee didn't run over dry areas.

<u>STEP 6 – Dry the remaining edges</u>

Once you're done with the squeegee you can dry the remaining edges of your window with a rag. You can find my ebook, "How to Start a Window Cleaning Business... With an Asset You Already Have" on Amazon.

There are six steps. You can see there are 3 stages within each of these 6 steps.

- Scrub - Scrape - Scrub
- Dry - Use a Squeegee to Dry

This is the first step. You will be able, if necessary, to remove any dirt or particles that you cannot scrub off. Next, remove all water from the window.

This is a very effective method to clean windows. It can be used to clean any type of window. You can also modify the six steps as you wish, or use them as a basis for your own method. There may be times when the window is not necessary to be scraped. This could be when the windows are not very dirty or there is film that would cause damage if it were. Instead of 6 steps, there will be 4 in these cases.

Scrub - Dry-Squeegee Dry

You might also be interested in the super swirl squeezegee technique. This is where the squeegee moves across the glass in fancy motions so that it does not need to be lifted off the glass. One motion is all that is required to complete the squeegee procedure.

There are many ways to speed up this technique. Also, there are window cleaners who can use the same or similar techniques.

This technique is not as fast as a water-fed pole, however, as you'll soon discover.

Chapter 2 - The water-fed pole and the parts

Now it is time to move on to the water-fed pole. This is why I wrote this book. It is called a water fed pole but there are many parts to it. There are four main parts to the pole, and I will list them in the order they appear.

The Water Filter

The water filter is the first. Its function is, as the name implies, to filter water. A water filter is necessary for cleaning windows with a water-fed pole. The water-fed pole leaves the window damp, unlike the traditional method, which requires you to remove any water from the windows with a squeegee. You then dry the edges using a towel. This is fine if the water has been purified. The glass will dry without any marks.

The water filter, when filled with water, is the largest part of the entire water-fed pole system. Although I don't know the details of water filters, they are likely to be similar to water filters used in kitchens to purify water. My water filter has resin, which I understand is what it needs to be.

Replaced once per year.
The water filter attaches directly to the tap. To help me get to work, I always bring a small piece of hose. It's handy for people who don't have hoses. A TDS meter, which is a device that measures the total dissolved solids (total dissolved solids), is also a tool I have. It allows me to determine how pure the water coming out of the filter is, and I can then be certain that it is working properly.
Water goes through the filter, and the water is purified on the other side. There is no waiting. It is very fast to get the water out of the other side. It must be filtered quickly. The second part of the water-fed pole is now complete. The water is then released from the filter and goes into ....

The Hose

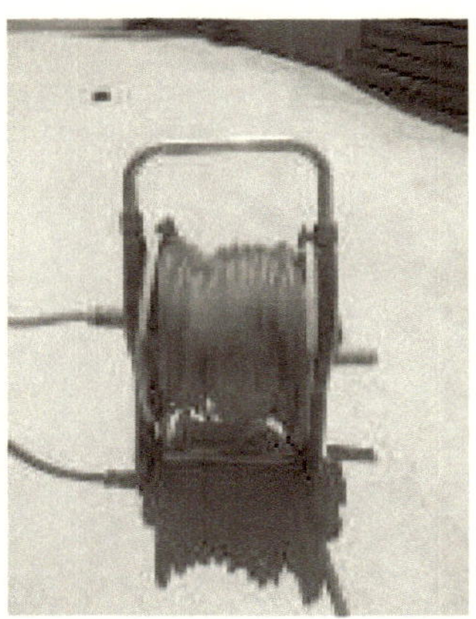

My hose measures 50m in length, but there are longer ones. This
ebook covers a 100-m hose. My 50m hose is long enough to clean
the entire exterior of a house with one tap. One example is that I
might be able clean two sides of a house using the 50 mhose. Then, I
can walk back to the tap and clean the 2 remaining sides in the
opposite direction.
Sometimes, I have to use two taps. This may help me avoid having to
drag my hose through difficult terrain such as steps, bushes, rocks,
etc. Although you can choose to use a longer hose than I did, 50m
seems adequate for me. Your job requirements and storage space will
determine which hose you choose. A 100-m hose will take up more
room than a 50-m hose.
The hose ends at ....

The Pole

You can see in the photo that my pole is approximately as tall as me when it is down. It fits easily in my Holden Astra Wagon.
My pole, when fully extended, measures 22 feet (roughly 7 meters) in length. It isn't the shortest, but it is quite short. It is sufficient length to fit into most 2nd-storey windows. It is rarely necessary to extend it fully to reach 2nd-storey windows. I don't work on buildings higher than 2 stories, but I have tried it on larger buildings and it can sometimes be enough to reach 3rd-storey windows. You can see my red pole at the center of the photo. It extends to the point that it touches the bottom of the third-storey window. Add the height of the user and it becomes clear that cleaning the windows on the third storey of this building with my pole is possible.

My pole measures 1.5m in length when it is unextended. The pole
will remain longer when fully extended than it is at rest. All poles,
however, are quite short at rest. My pole fits easily in the back seat
of my car. The poles are also heavier than the shorter ones, but they
are still relatively lightweight. Although you may feel sore in your
arms when first using them, once you get used to them and allow
your legs to do the majority of the work (as we'll discuss later), this
won't be a major problem.

Actually, the pole is the most costly part of the entire water-fed pole
system. The pole is connected to the brush by running the hose
through it at its lowest point.

The Brush

It looks very similar to the broom brush. The brush is different from a regular broom because it has a little bit of hose attached (yellow in this case). It is connected to the main line described above. The brush's hose then connects to 2 separate tubes or hoses (black in this case). These create jets at the top of your brush. When the tap is turned on, water flows through the tube and out at the jets.

Installing the water-fed pole

After you've been familiarized with the components of the water-fed pole, let us now go through how to set it up. We will then begin to view it as one unit.

Attach the water filter to your tap. This is not true. Attach the water filter to your garden hose.

Some houses and buildings don't have any garden hoses and so it is always handy to purchase and keep with you a small piece of garden hose, such as in the photo below. You will notice that that same piece of garden hose has been used in the photo above.

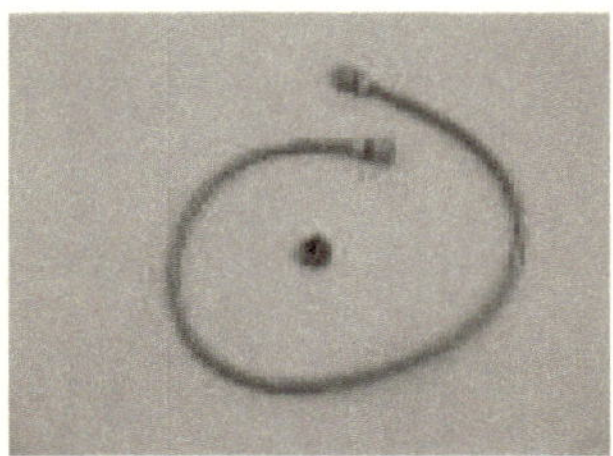

When the water filter is attached to the hose / tap, the next things to do is to attach the hose that you bought with your unit to the water filter.

Next roll out some of the hose. Now you can run the hose through the pole, attach the end of it to the bit of hose on the end of the brush, and then you can attach the brush to the top of the pole. Those steps are illustrated below.

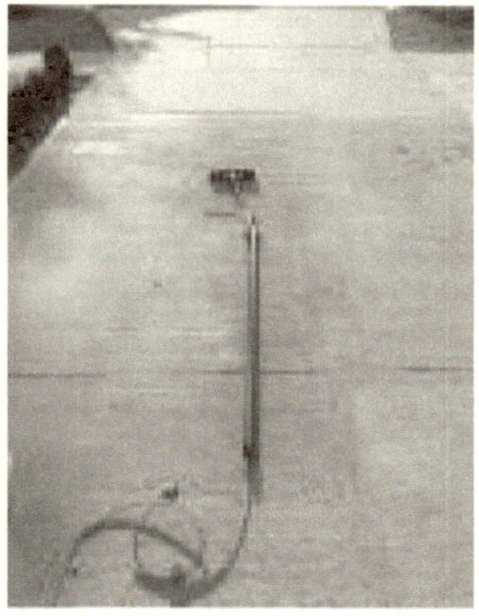

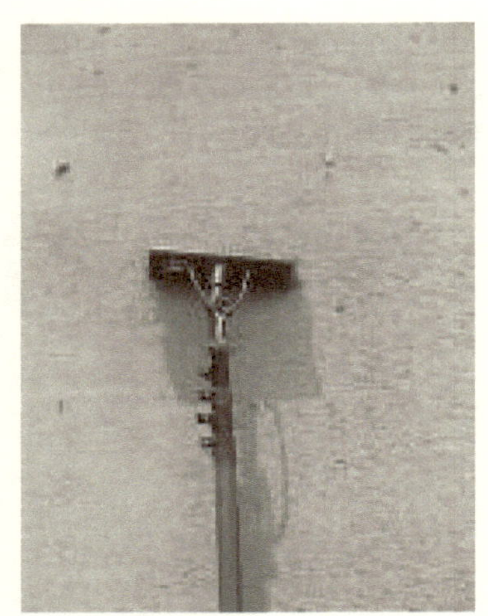

It's as simple as that. The water filter is connected to the tap (through a garden hose). The hose is connected to the water filter. The end of the hose is pushed through the pole, is connected to the bit of hose on the brush, and then the brush is secured to the pole. The photo below shows the water-fed pole as one connected unit, with the water filter and hose in the distance, and the pole sitting on the ground in the foreground.

Once you have installed your water-fed pole, you can start cleaning the windows by turning on the tap. You may also find a valve on the water filter. These must be turned on. The water flows through the filter and through the hose to the faucet. It then exits the 2 jets at top of the brush.
It is very beneficial to work in houses or buildings with good water pressure. The water pressure at the tap will determine the pressure at which the water comes out of the sprayers at the end. It will drip down the jets if the pressure is too low.

It is not sufficient to rinse the windows. The pressure should not be too high as it can splash onto the windows and make it impossible to rinse them effectively. It is best to let the water run out of the jets before it cascades down.

If the water pressure is low, even though you open the tap completely, the water may not flow as desired. If the water pressure at a tap is high, it will be possible to adjust it to achieve the desired pressure

It's easy to both extend the pole while the water is on and to also shorten it. It is just a sign that the pole is being extended.

It can be difficult to learn how to use new tools or equipment. This was my first experience with a water-fed pole. It was easy to learn and I am now comfortable with it. There are many models and brands. This unit is very basic for domestic window cleaning. You may need a different unit. It is likely that it will still be composed of the following 4 parts, regardless how different they may look: water filter, pole, pole, and brush.

<u>Youtube recommended videos:</u>
Add ons for the ultimate waterfed pole
Waterfed pole tips and tricks - fan jets vs pencil Reach -iT pole demo

Chapter 3: The water-fed pole is the method
Rinse and scrub.

6 steps were described in the first chapter on the traditional method of cleaning windows.

- Clean the window
- You can scrape the window
- Reopen the window.
- Two edges should be dried: side and top
- Use 2 strokes to clean the window.
- The rest of the edges can be dried

These 6 steps can be broken down into 2 phases with each having 3 steps.

- Scrub - Scrape - Scrub
- Dry - Use a Squeegee to Dry

The first stage removes dirt and particles from the windows. The second stage involves removing all of that and cleaning the window. There are two steps when you use the water-fed pole. They correspond to the 2 stages of the traditional method. These are the steps:

- Scrub
- Rinse

That's all. It's as easy as that. The **scrub** is the first step. It's the equivalent to the

scrape -of a conventional method. The second step is **rinse**
This is the dry equivalent to the dry-squeegee-dry method.
The water-fed pole works in the same way as the traditional method. The window will become very wet from the water-fed pole. You can then scrub it back.
You can go back and forth as many times as you want. The bristles on the brush are extremely effective in removing dirt from windows.

There is a way to use your brush in a different manner than the traditional method. The frame of the window is rarely cleaned when I use the traditional method. It may be wiped with a rag during the dry-squeegee drying stage, but it is rarely scrubbed.

It is best to clean the frames of windows before using a water-fed pole. This is because the second step of cleaning the window involves washing it. If the frames are dirty, the water that runs down them may pick up dirt and deposit it on the window.

The dry-squeegee drying stage of the traditional method has a different rinsing process. Dry-squeegee dry is the traditional method. This involves taking water off the window and drying it using both rags as well as a squeegee. The water-fed pole method's rinsing stage involves raising the brush from the window's surface and holding it at a distance of a few inches from glass. Let the water jets flow down the glass. The water will move down the glass and bring all dirt and bits to the bottom.

It is a good idea to move the brush horizontally across the window, while moving it downwards. You'll see tiny bits of glass and you can aim your jets towards them to direct them down the windowsill. You might find that some bits remain on a window after you have cleaned it. You can then repeat the process until you have removed all of the pieces.

It will not dry the same way as the traditional method, even if you have used the squeegee or rags to clean the windows. Instead, water will continue to drip down. This doesn't mean that water isn't important. It will dry clean once it has been purified. It will dry quickly if the sun is shining on it. It doesn't matter how wet your window looks after you have washed it. What matters is how thorough you scrubbed it and how thoroughly it was rinsed. The water-fed pole actually works better than the traditional method. Instead of six steps, there are only two. There are only two tools instead of four.

Step 1 - Scrub

Step 2 – Rinse

This brief description should make it clear that window cleaning using a water-fed pole to clean windows is more efficient than the traditional method. But is it as efficient as the traditional method? Good question. It is not possible to give you a definitive yes or no answer. However, it is worth explaining.

First, the water-fed pole works. It is definitely more of a "hope for the best" method than a "sure thing" method. It does clean windows. It is quite simple. It is obvious that most window cleaning is too much. Window cleaners tend to do more work than they should when cleaning windows. This is true for both water-fed pole and conventional methods.

Let me explain. A typical dirty window will have a thin layer of dust covering the entire window. There may also be some more severe marks on a specific section. Because most windows are not very dirty, it is easy to clean them most of all. Window cleaners don't usually clean all of the windows at once. They will clean only the most dirty parts and then clean the rest.

Instead, they treat each window as a single dirty window and give the entire surface the same treatment. The goal is to clean the entire window using a comprehensive, surface-wide cleaning method. They may use fine grade steel wool to remove stubborn marks.

Windows can be cleaned with the water-fed pole. The combination of the bristles and the water jets can make windows clean very effectively. They can sometimes not remove stubborn marks. I'll explain how to do that later. I want to assure you, for now, that the water-fed pole works.

Second-storey windows

Cleaning multi-storey buildings is where the water-fed pole's utility becomes especially apparent. Although I can only clean buildings up to 2 stories tall, water-fed poles are able to be used on taller buildings. As I said, my pole is 22 feet long. It measures approximately 7 meters in length. It can reach most second-floor windows, and sometimes even third-floor windows. There are longer poles and they can be used on tall buildings.

Depending on the job, the water-fed pole may be able to completely eliminate the need for a ladder. This saves a lot of time. It saves time climbing up and down ladders. It is possible to save all the time it takes to move a ladder around a building. It saves time getting the ladder off your vehicle and back on. As I'll explain, there will be times when you still need a ladder. It is not a good idea to get rid of a ladder. The water-fed pole drastically reduces the need for a ladder. I had two long ladders before I started using the water-fed pole. One I used frequently, the other only occasionally. The one I used frequently, I use now only occasionally. I no longer use the one I used to occasionally use. The ladder was sat on the back of my car while I cleaned a two-storey house.

A water-fed pole is safer than a ladder and it's more efficient. Recently, I met a window cleaner that I knew in a bank. He was walking on crutches. I had a good conversation with him. He was using crutches to walk because he fell from a ladder while cleaning a window. He would have been saved by a water-fed pole. A water-fed pole is unlikely to cause anyone to fall. It would have also saved him money, or should I say made him more money. He won't be able to work while he recovers from his injury. Needless to mention, I suggested to him that once he is able to work again, he should get a water-fed pole for himself.

After all that, it's important to mention how high windows can be cleaned.

It is much easier to clean a water-fed pole than it is to use conventional tools and a ladder. A ladder allows you to get up close and personal. You are limited in your ability to reach the window from a distance with a pole. This will not be an issue once you become proficient at using the water-fed pole. Remember what I just

said. Window cleaning can be overwhelming. You can clean the windows well from a distance if you give it a thorough clean by pressing the brush against the glass. You may see any marks or stains that you didn't clean when you enter the house. You can always remove the ladder if it is absolutely necessary.
The advantages are definitely more important than the disadvantages, I can tell you that. No question. It is worth it.

Multiple panes for vertical relationships

Water-fed poles can be used in a number of useful ways. The photo below shows a simple sliding glass window. There are two panes of glass at each end. This type of window can be cleaned with a water-fed pole. Water will drip from the top panes onto your bottom panes if you don't clean them all at once. This is not ideal. The bottom panes could then be stained by any dirty water that drips down from the top panes. Although it may not occur, there is always the possibility.

The best course of action is to allow water from the top panes to finish dripping before cleaning the bottom panes. Whenever I clean a building that has lots of windows with top and bottom panes, I first go around and clean all the top panes on each of the windows. Then when I revisit each window in the same order, the dripping from the top pains has stopped, and I can go around and clean the bottom panes.

The correct stance

When you use the water-fed pole, don't just rely on your arms to do the work, or you'll often get extremely sore arms. Instead, use the strength from your legs and hips and much as possible. You can see in the photograph below that I have one leg in front of the other. One technique is to step forward and step back, rather than move yours arms up and down. It will move the brush up and down the window just as well, and you won't get so sore and tired, so you'll do a better job.

Water consumption

Using the conventional method, all you need to do is fill a bucket with water and that is often enough to clean an entire house. You may empty and refill the bucket in order to put clean water in, but you still use a tiny amount of water. On the other hand, using a water-fed pole does mean that you will use more water as water is continuously coming out of the jets.

However, the amount of water being used is not excessive, and there are ways of keeping it to a minimum. Firstly, you can adjust the tap so that the water coming out of the jets is no more than you think you need. Secondly, if you need to stop working for a few moments to for example answer your phone, simply turn the tap off. As well as the main tap, I have a tap on my hose near the end that I can turn off, saving me the trouble of having to walk all the way to the tap if I'm far away. There is also an attachment you can buy that sits on the pole that enables you to stop the flow of water. Also keep in mind that the water you are using is not disappearing, it is not being lost. It is simply being moved, and sometimes changing form, such as when it is being evaporated. You are also purifying it, as opposed to using chemicals with it.

<u>Recommended youtube videos:</u>

How to do a first clean with WFP
WFP class – basic residential technique
Waterfed pole tips and technique – the basics of WFP cleaning WFP

class – commercial windows basic technique

Water-fed pole techniques w/ Josh Corey

Chapter 4 : The water-fed pole – the challenges
There are 3 major variables that determine how easy it is to clean windows
with a water-fed pole.
1. Water pressure
2. Dirtiness of the windows
3. Hydrophobic windows

Let's look at these one at a time.

Water pressure

The water pressure does not have anything to do the pole and windows. It simply indicates how strong the water pressure coming out of the tap. The water pressure will determine how forcefully it comes out of your tap. The water should not drip down too quickly, but it shouldn't splash against windows. You want it to project gently like it does at many fountains.

You may see tiny particles stuck to windows after cleaning them. These particles may not be able to be pushed down if the water pressure is low. It will be easier to wash these particles from the window and rinse it well if the water pressure is high.

Water pressure is rarely an issue in my experience. Sometimes, one tap in a house has higher water pressure than the other. In these cases, I use the tap with the highest water pressure.

Window dirt

The more dirty a window is, it will be harder to clean. First clean
windows are more likely to get dirty. When you clean the windows
for the first-time. These windows are usually dirty and have not been
cleaned in a while. If you're cleaning a building or house that was
last cleaned less than a year ago, the dirt will not be as severe and it
will be much easier to clean. A repeat clean can be done with a pole.
The water-fed pole might not be sufficient if your windows are very
dirty. The more you scrub, the cleaner your windows will be. This
will be covered in greater detail in the next chapter. I will say for
now that if you are having trouble getting the windows clean using
the pole alone, you can always use the traditional method to get
additional tools.

A scraper is an effective tool for cleaning windows. Fine grade steel
wool is another powerful tool for cleaning windows. It can remove
stubborn marks very effectively. Fine grade steel wool should only
be used on windows. For stubborn marks, you can use coarser grades
of steel wool.

It doesn't really matter if the windows take a bit longer to clean. You
will do a great job. You are more likely to be referred by repeat
customers if you do a great job. If you have repeat business, it will
make the building easier to clean and you won't require any
additional tools.

Hydrophobic windows

Hydrophilia, hydrophobia. These terms sound more psychological than the terms you'll find in a book about window cleaning. Let me tell you. "Hydro", obviously, means water. "Philia" means love. Phobia is fear, aversion, or dislike. Anglophile is a term that refers to a love for England and all things English. You may also have heard the term "Anglophile", which refers to a love of England and all things English. Hydrophilic means that you love water. While hydrophobic is a dislike of it.

It is very easy to wet a window that is hydrophilic. It is easy to wet a window because the water spreads over it. The water does not evaporate or drain off. A hydrophobic window, on the other hand refuses to get wet. It repels water, no matter how much you pour on it. It seems that the water runs down narrow channels in the window. Hydrophilia and hydrophobia are not two distinct categories. They refer to a continuum. Window tend to fall somewhere on the continuum. It could be very hydrophilic or extremely hydrophobic, depending on its purpose.

It is not clear why windows behave in this manner. However, I have found that sliding windows that have a screen in front tend to be hydrophobic. The side without the screen tends not to have that problem.

A window cleaner who uses a water-fed pole can clean hydrophilic windows with ease. When you use the water-fed pole, these windows are easy to love. It is very simple to clean them thoroughly as the water flows down the window steadily. The dirty water drains out of the entire window. If you keep wetting it, you will know it is the recently used water.

Hydrophobic windows can cause problems for window cleaners who use a water-fed pole. Hydrophobic windows won't get wet. The water doesn't get spread across the glass. It seems that the water runs down rivers and channels. Hydrophobic windows are those that are resistant to water.

It is very difficult to clean the windows as it is impossible to get water to run off the entire surface.

This may not be a problem if the window wasn't very dirty. It is important to take your time and rinse the window slowly, at least

twice. It is possible to not clean the entire window if the glass was dirty from the beginning. You will notice little marks when the window dries. These aren't marks you left on the window originally and that you didn't clean. They are new. They form when the dirt you have previously removed from the window is mixed with the water that you use to clean it. Then, the window is dried again.
Sometimes, these spots are not too big of a deal. They may not be obvious at all, so you have two options: a) go over the window again hoping for better luck; b) wait for the window drying completely and then use fine grade steel wool to remove the spots. It is important to be aware. It can be annoying. It can be a good idea to take a look at all the windows after a job is done to ensure that there are not too many.

Interactions among the three
These three factors, water pressure, dirtiness and
hydrophilia/hydrophobia, interact with one another. A water-fed pole
will require good water pressure, a window with hydrophilia, and a
window that's not too dirty. These conditions will make it easy to
clean your window. It will be harder to clean windows if there is
poor water pressure and the window is very dirty or
hydrophobic. You won't find yourself in extreme situations in either
of these areas very often. Hydrophobia can be overcome by good
water pressure.
Hydrophobia isn't likely to be an issue if the window isn't very
dirty. As I mentioned before, you can always look over the problem
and use additional tools. You may decide not to use the water-fed
pole in some cases.

<u>Recommended youtube videos</u>

Hydrophobic to hydrophilic with bronze wool 4 months later
Waterfed pole training: what causes spots when pure water window cleaning
How to stop window from spotting

Chapter 5: Blended methods – the well-rounded window cleaner

Be holistic – not polistic
Even though the subject of this ebook is window cleaning with a water-fed pole, I began it with a chapter on the conventional method of cleaning windows. It was important to include the description of the conventional method of cleaning windows. Firstly, the water-fed pole cannot be used in all situations. It cannot be used inside buildings, and on some occasions, it may not be the most appropriate tool on the outside of buildings either. Secondly, the conventional method and the water-fed pole method shouldn't be treated as mutually exclusive methods, even though they are quite distinct. Some aspects of the conventional approach can be incorporated with the use of the water-fed pole.

The water-fed pole is a very impressive tool. It's definitely a game changer. Make no mistake. When I started using it, I felt a sense of regret at the amount of time I had wasted cleaning windows with the conventional method, when I could have been much more easily and speedily cleaning them with the water-fed pole. I began by using the pole automatically and without question on all external windows. That is probably natural and understandable. Whenever a new technology comes along, it makes old technologies seem obsolete and even silly, and the tendency is to embrace the new technology and forget the old one.
I was reminded of the scene in an Indiana Jones movie when Indiana Jones was in a conflict situation where he was confronted by a combatant wielding a knife. The combatant started waving the knife around in preparation for a duel in which he expected to be victorious. Instead, even before the duel began, Indiana Jones pulled out a gun and shot and killed the man. He did so in a manner that was dismissive and casual and that made the combatant's overtures appear laughable. The combatant had been confronted with a superior technology – a gun, and the gun easily beat the knife. It could do what the knife couldn't do.

The water-fed pole is a bit like a gun, and the conventional window cleaning tools are a bit like a knife. The water-fed pole can enable the window cleaner to achieve a speed that far outpaces even the most skilful window cleaner using conventional tools and the fancy super swirl technique.

Nevertheless, even though a gun is a far most advanced and deadly weapon than a knife, we still have knives, and knives can still do things that guns can't. Similarly, some of the conventional window cleaning tools can still do things that the water-fed pole cannot, and they all have a place in the window cleaner's toolkit.

I have now been using the water-fed pole for about 4 months, and I have now integrated it into my window cleaning. I have gotten good at using it, and I have gotten good at making judgements about when to use it and when to leave it in the car. I have also gotten good at making judgements about when and which conventional windows cleaning tools to use alongside it. Instead of using it on external windows in an exclusive sort of manner such as an Indiana Jones assuming he only needs to carry a gun and no longer has use for a knife, I know that there are times when it's not the best tool for the job, when its disadvantages outweigh its advantages.

As recently as yesterday I did a job which may have seemed on the surface to have been the perfect job for the water-fed pole, as it was a 2-storey external window only job. However, I chose not to use the water-fed pole at all. The job was the external windows of two 2-storey townhouses that faced each other. The 2 townhouses were identical to each other.

I noticed immediately that they each had a second storey window that I wasn't going to be able to reach front-on standing on the ground, as they each had a section of roof in front on them. If I tried to clean them with the water-fed pole from the ground, it was going to be from a very awkward angle. I concluded that in order to make sure I cleaned it properly, I going to have to climb onto the roof. As a result, I was going to have to get my ladder out to get onto the roof whether I used the water-fed pole or not. This was also a first time job, and the windows were very dirty. It was also a relatively small job, so the water-fed pole wasn't going to save me a hell of a lot of time anyway.

Taking all these factors into account I decided immediately that I wasn't going to use the water-fed pole. I completed each townhouse in an hour using the conventional approach and made $200 altogether. Had I used the water-fed pole, I may have saved a little bit of time, but not a great deal, and I possibly wouldn't have done quite as good a job, and if so I may have reduced my chances of getting repeat business from those customers.

There are other occasions. There are occasions when it may not be best to choose between one method *or* the other. Sometimes it may be advisable to combine the two. Sometimes I combine the speed of the pole with the thoroughness of some of the conventional tools. I cleaned a house not long ago for which I used both the water-fed pole and the scraper on the external windows. I scrubbed the windows with the water-fed pole, them scraped them with the scraper, scrubbed them again briefly with the pole before rinsing them. In other words, I used a **scrub – scrape – scrub – rinse** approach. Some of the windows were a little high up so that they couldn't be reached by hand from the ground. I was even able to scrape those slightly higher windows by putting my scraper on the end of an ordinary pole.

There are window cleaners who avoid using scrapers altogether, for fear of scratching windows. This is a legitimate fear, as scrapers can scratch windows. You would need to be particularly careful if you use one on the end of an ordinary pole as I've described, as you will be less sensitive to whether you're scratching a window than you would be if you're actually holding the scraper with your hand. (See my first ebook "How to start a window cleaning business ... with an asset you already have" for in depth information on how to use scrapers effectively and to minimise the chances of scratching windows with it)

A tool that can be a good alternative to scrapers is fine grade steel wool. Fine grade steel wool is an absolute dream tool for window cleaners, and it is extremely cheap. Courser grades of steel wool will scratch windows, and must never be used. However, fine grade steel wool does not scratch windows and it often cleans them even better than scrapers do. The window cleaner to whom this book is dedicated likes to carry a bit of fine grade steel wool in his pocket when he is using the water-fed pole. When he notices a stubborn stain on a window that is not being removed by the brush on the end of his water-fed pole, he pulls out the piece of steel wool in his pocket and uses it to remove the stain. Then he resumes using the water-fed pole. Sometimes I do the same, and on some occasions, such as when frames or tracks need a wipe, I actually carry a rag on my shoulder whilst using the water-fed pole. In short, 3 of the conventional window cleaning tools – scraper, steel wool, and rags – can each be incorporated with the water-fed pole for better outcomes. The bottom line is, be wary of any "one size fits all" or "one method cleans all" attitudes to window cleaning. There are so many different situations, and if you have a broad array of tools in your repertoire, you can combine them in ways to suit different situations.

Ladder ladder on the wall – are you necessary after all?
I mentioned earlier that the water-fed pole dramatically cuts down on the
need for a ladder. This is absolutely true. As I said before, whereas I used to
use one ladder frequently and another occasionally, I now only use one
ladder occasionally. I also mentioned a recent job on 2 storey townhouses
for which I chose to use the conventional method instead of the pole, and
which involved the use of my ladder.

Sometimes I use the water-fed pole, but still need to use a ladder. In the example pictured below I needed to use the ladder to get onto the platform by the front door. As I was using the water-fed pole on the rest of the external windows, it was less trouble to carry the water-fed pole up the ladder than to drop it and get my conventional tools out.

There are also other occasions. I have had occasions where I was able to take the screen of a second storey out from a window from inside the house, and was able to clean the outside of the window with the water-fed pole, but was then unable to put the screen back in from the inside. In other words, I could take the screen out from the inside, but was unable to put in back in from the inside. I had to get the ladder out just to put the screen back in the window, because I had to do it from the outside.

So the answer to the question at the start of this section is "yes." You will still need a ladder. If you're a domestic window cleaner, I wouldn't rely on using the customer's ladder, because some customers don't have ladders. Sometimes you can clean or touch up a second storey window from inside the house, especially if it's a sliding window. But if you're serious about being a window cleaner, I wouldn't try to get away with these sorts of chancy techniques. One day you'll end up risking your safety, and you should put your safety first.

Go out and get yourself a good ladder. I recommend you look at Chapter 6 of my first ebook on window cleaning. That ebook, which I have referred to a few times in this ebook, is called "How to start a window cleaning business

... with an asset you already have." You will find it on Amazon under the keywords "window cleaning" and you will also find it on the following website if you want a pdf version that you can easily print out: www.windowcleaningasset.com

Transforma ladder

Chapter 6 in that ebook is called "Climbing the ladder." In it I describe a ladder which I refer to by its brand name : Transforma ladder. It is called "transforma" ladder because it can be transformed. It can be lengthened and shortened, and it can converted from an A-frame ladder to an extension ladder and back again. The ladder is in the 2 photographs above and the photograph below. In the 2 photographs above it is in the form of an extension ladder, and in the photograph below it is in the form of an A-frame ladder. That's right. It is the same ladder that is in each of the photos.

As you can see in the photo now above, each side can be set at different lengths, which can come in handy in instances such as when a window is in front of steps, as you can see. Altogether, taking into account all the different lengths that each side of the ladder can assume, and the fact that it can be either an A-frame or an extension ladder, that particular ladder can actually assume the form of more than 30 different ladders. So when I have that ladder on the top of my car, it's a bit like having 30 ladders on my car. However, not only is this ladder able to be converted or "transforma'd" into so many different ladders, at its resting form it is very small and compact, and can sit neatly on a very small car. When I started window cleaning I was driving a Mazda 121, which is an extremely small car. The transforma ladder sat quite easily on it, and did not look out of place. I now drive a Holden Astra Wagon, which is a bigger car than a Mazda 121, but is by no means a heavy commercial vehicle. Needless to say, the ladder now looks very much at home on my new car.

The take home message is that if you want to be a window cleaner, even if you want to use a water-fed pole, I still recommend you buy a ladder, as it will come in handy. You may not need it as much as you would otherwise, but it will still come in very handy, especially if it's as convertible as the transforma ladder I've illustrated and described. If you buy the transforma ladder or one with a similar design, it may end up being the only ladder you need to buy as a window cleaner. Before I used the pole, as I mentioned earlier, in addition to the transforma ladder I also had a very long extension ladder that I used occasionally. I never use that now. So buying a water-fed pole may not save you from buying a ladder, but it may save you from buying two.

The skyscraper is the limit

When I bought my water-fed pole, I did so knowing that I only clean 2 storey buildings at the highest. As a result, I only bought a 22 foot water-fed pole.

This is by no means the shortest water-fed pole that you can purchase, but it is one of the shortest. As you can see from the photograph above, you can purchase much longer water-fed poles, and you can clean much higher than 2 storeys with them. As far as I am aware, you can go as high as 6 storeys with them. For windows higher than that, you will need scissor lifts or rope access.

Don't be limited by my limitations. I concentrate on residential work, and there are very few houses that are taller than 2 stories. However, if you wish to take things further than me, or should I say higher than me, then there is nothing to stop you.

Getting more efficient on the inside
Before I used the water-fed pole, I would generally take longer to clean the outside of a house than to clean the inside. This was especially so in the case of 2 storey houses, as I would need to use a ladder on the outside, whereas I normally wouldn't need to use one on the inside.

Since I have been using the water-fed pole, my experience has often been the opposite. I have been able to clean the external windows faster than the internal windows, sometimes twice as fast, even on 2 storey houses. This hasn't always been my experience. Each job is different, and there are so many variables that can tilt things one way or the other. However, it can happen.
This increased efficiency on the outside has naturally led me to wonder whether any efficiency gains can be made on the inside. One cannot bring the water-fed pole inside the house for obvious reasons. However, there may still be ways of increasing efficiency on the inside.
Here are a few ideas. To explain, let's look back at the conventional method of cleaning windows that was described in chapter 1. There I outlined a 6 step process:
Scrub – Scrape – Scrub – Dry – Squeegee – Dry
Often windows on the inside are not especially dirty. It may not be necessary to go through each of these steps. As I briefly mentioned in Chapter 1, it may be possible to eliminate some of these steps without making any difference to the outcome. In other words, some of the steps may be redundant on windows that aren't particularly dirty, or they may be able to be modified. Here are a few ideas.

1. Scrub – Dry – Squeegee – Dry

There is often no need to use a scraper on internal windows. Sometimes, it's even destructive, such as on window films, and must be avoided at all costs. However, even if a window does not have a window film, ask yourself: "do I really need to scrape this window?" If not, don't scrape it. By eliminating the scrape stage, you'll also eliminate the need for the second scrub stage. Six steps have already been reduced to four, saving you a lot of time. There may be one or two internal windows in the house that do need to be scraped. That's fine. But why scrape all the internal windows, if most of them don't need it?

2. Scrub with fine grade steel wool – Dry – Squeegee – Dry

I recently picked up this idea from another window cleaner, and I can't believe I didn't think of it myself. Fine grade steel wool is extremely effective at cleaning stubborn stains and smears off windows that often even scrapers haven't removed. I had always used fine grade steel wool at the end of the 6 stage process, to do touch-ups. It had effectively been at stage 7 process for me.

But here's the idea. Why not use fine grade steel wool as the tool for the number 1 stage. Cut off a large clump of it, plunge it into your bucket, and scrub the window with it. If you do this, you won't need to use a scraper even for the dirty windows, because the fine grade steel wool is so effective.

Please note: just like the case for scraper, do not use fine grade steel wool on window films as it will scratch them.

3. Scrub – Squeegee – Dry

Here I've taken even another step out of the process, the first drying step. If you're really neat with the squeegee, you may not really need it. If you have a good cleaning chemical with a surfactant in it, it will help hold the water to the glass and prevent it from dripping down too quickly. This will make it easier for you to squeegee the window. Now you've gone from 6 steps down to 3.

4. Scrub with fine grade steel wool – Squeegee with the "wagtail squeegee" using the "super swirl" method - Dry

I never really mastered the super swirl technique. It's the fancy technique you have probably seen window cleaners cleaning shopfronts using.

They make a fancy "S" shape with the squeegee, and can clean even a large window with the one motion. They never have to take the squeegee off the glass, dry it, and put it back on the glass again.

I think the reason I never mastered the technique and tended to avoid using it is because I found it difficult to perform with the squeegee I was using. It had never been impressed on me that there is a squeegee specifically designed to facilitate the technique. It is designed to rotate with just the slightest turn of the wrist. I only bought my first one today, and I'm guessing that it's going to become a valued part of my toolkit.

Recommended Youtube videos on the wagtail squeegee: Wagtail demo

& ecover review by Wayne

Window cleaning with wagtail tools

We've now gone from 6 steps to 3, and even shortened the 2nd step. With the combination of the water-fed pole on the external windows, and a rationalised method on the internal windows, you're ready to become an extremely efficient window cleaner, even without too much experience.